Pebble®
Bilingüe/ Plus
Bilingual

Deportes y actividades/Sports and Activities

¡Vamos a jugar al béisbol!

Let's Play Baseball!

por/by Terri DeGezelle

Editora consultora/Consulting Editor: Gail Saunders-Smith, PhD

Consultora/Consultant: Kymm Ballard, MA
Consultora de Educación Física, Atletismo y Medicina Deportiva
Departamento de Instrucción Pública de Carolina del Norte/
Physical Education, Athletics, and Sports Medicine Consultant
North Carolina Department of Public Instruction

CAPSTONE PRESS
a capstone imprint

Pebble Plus is published by Capstone Press,
1710 Roe Crest Drive, North Mankato, Minnesota 56003.
www.capstonepub.com

 Books published by Capstone Press are manufactured with paper
containing at least 10 percent post-consumer waste.

Library of Congress Cataloging-in-Publication Data
DeGezelle, Terri, 1955–
  ¡Vamos a jugar al béisbol! = Let's play baseball! / by Terri DeGezelle.
    p. cm.—(Pebble plus Deportes y actividades/Sports and activities)
  Includes index.
  Summary: "Simple text and photographs present the skills, equipment, and safety concerns of playing baseball—in both
English and Spanish"—Provided by publisher.
  ISBN 978-1-4296-8247-3 (library binding)
  1. Baseball—Juvenile literature. I. Title. II. Title: Let's play baseball!
  GV867.5.D443 2012
  796.357—dc23

Editorial Credits
Heather Adamson, editor; Strictly Spanish, translation services; Kia Adams, designer; Eric Manske, bilingual book
    designer; Kelly Garvin, photo researcher; Kathy McColley, production specialist

Photo Credits
All photos Capstone Press/ TJ Thoraldson Digital Photography except page 13, Getty Images/Jake Rajs and page 15,
    Corbis/David Madison/zefa.

The author thanks Chris Biehn for sharing his knowledge of baseball.

Note to Parents and Teachers

The Deportes y actividades/Sports and Activities set supports national physical education
standards related to recognizing movement forms and exhibiting a physically active lifestyle. This
book describes and illustrates baseball in both English and Spanish. The images support early
readers in understanding the text. The repetition of words and phrases helps early readers learn
new words. This book also introduces early readers to subject-specific vocabulary words, which
are defined in the Glossary section. Early readers may need assistance to read some words and to
use the Table of Contents, Glossary, Internet Sites, and Index sections of the book.

Printed in the United States of America in North Mankato, Minnesota.
102011   006405CGS12

Table of Contents

Tabla de contenidos

Playing Baseball

Catch, throw, hit, run,
score! Friends play
baseball together.

Juguemos al béisbol

¡Atrapa, lanza, golpea,
corre, anota! Los amigos
juegan juntos al béisbol.

Teams take turns at bat.
The pitcher throws the ball.
The batter tries to hit the
ball with a bat.

Los equipos se turnan al bate.
El lanzador lanza la pelota.
El bateador trata de golpear
la pelota con un bate.

Batters run to bases
after they hit the ball.
They score runs by
touching all the bases.

Los bateadores corren
a las bases después
de golpear la pelota.
Ellos anotan carreras
al tocar todas las bases.

The fielding team tries
to catch the batted ball.
They throw it. They try
to tag the runner out.

El equipo del campo trata de
atrapar la pelota bateada. Ellos
la lanzan. Ellos tratan de tocar al
corredor para que quede fuera.

Equipment

Baseball fields have three bases and a home plate. They make a diamond shape.

Equipo

Los campos de béisbol tienen tres bases y un *home plate*. Forman un diamante.

408ft.

COPYTEX

BUD LIGHT

385ft.

13

Baseball bats are made from
strong wood or metal.
They are built tough
to hit baseballs hard.

Los bates de béisbol están hechos
de madera dura o metal.
Son de construcción fuerte
para golpear duro a las
pelotas de béisbol.

Safety

Players wear helmets to protect their heads. They also wear caps to shield their eyes from the sun.

Seguridad

Los jugadores usan cascos para proteger sus cabezas. Ellos también usan gorras para proteger sus ojos del sol.

Players use leather gloves
to catch baseballs.
Then the ball does not
hurt their hands.

Los jugadores usan guantes
de cuero para atrapar pelotas
de béisbol. De esa manera, la
pelota no les lastima las manos.

Having Fun

Come hit the ball
and run the bases.
Let's play baseball!

Vamos a divertirnos

Ven, golpea la pelota
y corre las bases.
¡Vamos a jugar al béisbol!

Glossary

base—a bag or plate marking one of the four corners of a baseball diamond; runners must make it around all the bases without getting tagged out to score a run

diamond—a shape with four equal sides and two pairs of angles; baseball diamonds are actually squares that look like diamonds

out—ending a batter's attempt to score by catching a batter's hit, tagging a runner with the ball, or throwing the ball to a base before the runner reaches it; after three outs, the teams switch batting and fielding

pitcher—the player who throws the ball over home plate; in beginning leagues, a coach may be the pitcher

protect—to keep safe

Internet Sites

FactHound offers a safe, fun way to find Internet sites related to this book. All of the sites on FactHound have been researched by our staff.

Here's all you do:

Visit *www.facthound.com*

Type in this code: 9781429682473

Super-cool stuff!

Check out projects, games and lots more at
www.capstonekids.com

Glosario

la base—una bolsa o plato que marca uno de los cuatro rincones del diamante de béisbol; los corredores deben correr completamente alrededor de las bases sin que los agarren fuera de la base para anotar una carrera

el diamante—una figura con cuatro lados iguales y dos pares de ángulos; los diamantes de béisbol son en realidad cuadrados que se parecen a diamantes

fuera—finalizar el intento de un bateador para anotar al atrapar el bateo de un bateador, tocando a un jugador con la pelota, o lanzando la pelota a una base antes que el corredor llegue a esta; después de tres eliminaciones, los equipos intercambian el bateo y el juego en el campo

el lanzador—el jugador que lanza la pelota sobre el *home plate*; en las ligas de novatos, el entrenador puede que sea el lanzador

proteger—mantener seguro

Sitios de Internet

FactHound brinda una forma segura y divertida de encontrar sitios de Internet relacionados con este libro. Todos los sitios en FactHound han sido investigados por nuestro personal.

Esto es todo lo que tienes que hacer:

Visita *www.facthound.com*

Ingresa este código: 9781429682473

¡Algo súper divertido! Hay proyectos, juegos y mucho más en **www.capstonekids.com**

Index

Índice